VERONA
Tour Guide
2025

Darius Spencer

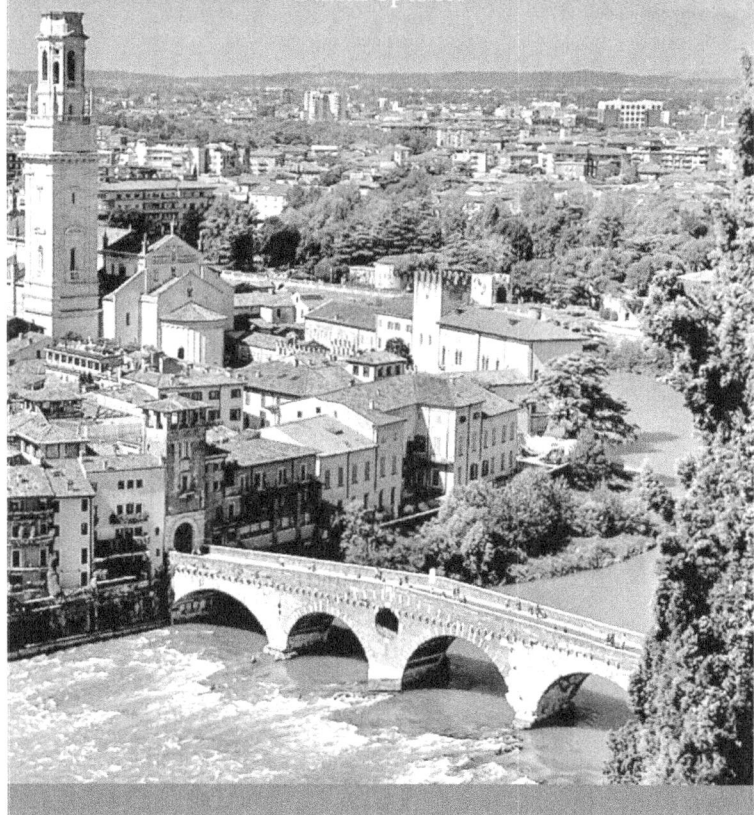

Verona Tour Guide 2025

TABLE OF CONTENT

CHAPTER 1:

DISCOVER VERONA'S RICH HISTORY

Uncover The Stories Behind Verona's Ancient Roman Ruins And Medieval Architecture

Verona's ancient Roman ruins and medieval architecture offer a captivating glimpse into the city's rich history and cultural evolution. The historic center of Verona has been recognized as a UNESCO World Heritage site, showcasing its extraordinary architectural and artistic heritage. One of the most significant remnants of Roman influence is the Verona Arena, an impressive amphitheater built in 30 AD. Originally constructed for gladiatorial contests, this architectural marvel can seat up to 15,000 spectators and is still used today for concerts and opera performances, particularly during the summer opera festival. The arena's structure is remarkable for its three concentric tiers of stone, standing nearly 30 meters high, making it one of the best-preserved Roman amphitheaters in existence.

To truly appreciate the grandeur of the Arena, consider joining a guided tour, which typically costs around $12 and includes skip-the-line access. The tours are available in multiple languages and last about an hour, giving you detailed insights into its history and significance. You can book tours online through the Verona Arena website or purchase tickets at the entrance, which is located at Piazza Bra, 1, 37121 Verona, Italy. The arena is open from 9 AM to 7 PM, but it's best to visit earlier in the day to avoid crowds.

Another highlight of Verona's Roman heritage is the Porta Borsari, an ancient city gate that dates back to the 1st century AD. Once serving as a primary entry point into the city, this well-preserved gate features stunning Corinthian columns and intricate carvings. Admission is free, and you can easily find it at Via Porta Borsari, 37121 Verona, Italy. Nearby, the Roman Theatre stands as a testament to the city's dramatic past, dating back to the 1st century BC. This theater could accommodate about 5,000 spectators and is surrounded by picturesque views of the Adige River. Visiting the Roman Theatre costs approximately $10, which also grants access to the adjoining archaeological museum. It's located at Via Ponte Pietra, 1, 37121 Verona, Italy, and is open from 10 AM to 6 PM.

Exploring these sites can be a delightful experience, especially if you wander through the surrounding areas where charming cafes and local shops dot the streets. Be sure to stop by Piazza delle Erbe, the former Roman forum, which is one of the oldest and most vibrant squares in Verona, bustling with activity. Here, you'll find a vibrant market selling everything from fresh produce to handmade crafts, and you can enjoy a coffee at one of the outdoor terraces while soaking in the stunning medieval architecture around you.

Explore The Significance Of Juliet's Balcony And Its Ties To Shakespeare's Timeless Tale

No visit to Verona is complete without experiencing Juliet's Balcony, a romantic spot that brings Shakespeare's tragic love story to life. Nestled in a courtyard of the Casa di Giulietta, this iconic balcony draws thousands of visitors eager to take in the ambiance of one of literature's most beloved tales. While the tale of Romeo and Juliet is fictional, the connection to Verona has made it a vital part of the city's cultural identity. The balcony itself is a stunning example of 13th-century architecture, and it's a place where lovers from all around the world come to pay tribute to the idea of star-crossed love.

Visiting Juliet's Balcony is free, but if you want to gain deeper insights into the location's history and the legend behind it, consider a guided tour for about $15, which includes entry to the museum. The Casa di Giulietta is located at Via Cappello, 23, 37121 Verona, Italy, and is open daily from 9 AM to 7 PM. The courtyard features a bronze statue of

Juliet, and tradition holds that touching her right breast brings good luck in love. You can also leave a message on the walls of the courtyard, a practice that has become a popular way for visitors to express their hopes and dreams.

In addition to the balcony, the museum offers a fascinating collection of artifacts, including letters and memorabilia from visitors, further enriching the experience. The museum ticket grants access to the entire building, which features rooms that reflect the lifestyle and traditions of the time. If you visit in the summer months, be prepared for large crowds, as this is peak tourist season. Try to arrive early in the morning or later in the afternoon for a more intimate experience.

The surrounding streets of Verona are lined with shops selling unique souvenirs, including love locks that couples can affix to nearby railings as a symbol of their commitment. After your visit, take a leisurely stroll through Piazza dei Signori, just a short walk away, where you can find historical statues, beautiful architecture, and cozy cafes, perfect for sipping an espresso or enjoying a gelato while reflecting on the stories you've just uncovered.

Delve Into The History Of The Verona Arena, One Of The Best-Preserved Ancient Structures In The World

The Verona Arena is not only an architectural marvel but also a cultural beacon that has stood the test of time. Built in 30 AD, this magnificent amphitheater reflects the ingenuity of Roman engineering and has served various purposes throughout its history. Originally designed for gladiatorial contests and public spectacles, the arena has hosted countless events, evolving from its original purpose to become one of the most important opera venues in the world. The stunning acoustics of the arena allow for extraordinary performances that captivate audiences, drawing opera lovers from all over the globe.

The Verona Arena's summer opera festival is a must-see event, showcasing world-class performances against the backdrop of this ancient structure. Tickets for the opera vary in price, ranging from $20 to $300, depending on the seating area and the specific production. Performances usually run from June to September, and you can check the Arena di Verona website for schedules and ticket availability. Attending an opera here is an unforgettable experience, as the night sky adds an enchanting ambiance to the performances.

In addition to opera, the Arena has also hosted concerts featuring renowned artists across various genres, making it a cultural hub that appeals to all. If you are visiting outside of the opera season, consider attending one of the many concerts held throughout the year, as the arena offers a unique atmosphere that enhances any performance. You can find the venue at Piazza Bra, 1, 37121 Verona, Italy, and it is open for visitors to explore daily from 9 AM to 7 PM.

To maximize your experience at the Arena, consider booking a guided tour that includes behind-the-scenes access, allowing you to learn more about its rich history and architectural features. These tours typically last about an hour and cost around $25, providing an in-depth understanding of this historic venue. Be sure to check out the impressive stonework and the ancient remains that give insight into the building's construction.

In conclusion, Verona's ancient Roman ruins and medieval architecture, along with the enchanting stories of Juliet and the grandeur of the Verona Arena, create a captivating tapestry of history and culture. The city is a treasure trove of experiences that allow visitors to immerse themselves in its rich past while enjoying the vibrancy of contemporary Italian life. From exploring the intricacies of ancient architecture to celebrating timeless love stories, Verona offers a unique and unforgettable journey for travelers eager to connect with its heritage. Whether you're an art enthusiast, a history buff, or a romantic at heart, Verona invites you to uncover its stories and create your own memories in this timeless Italian city.

CHAPTER 2:

WANDER THE CHARMING STREETS OF VERONA

Stroll Through Picturesque Piazzas Filled With Lively Cafes And Shops

Verona is a city that invites you to explore its enchanting piazzas, each bustling with life and charm. One of the most vibrant spots is Piazza delle Erbe, a lively market square that captures the essence of Italian culture. Here, locals and tourists alike mingle among the stalls selling fresh produce, local delicacies, and handmade crafts. The piazza is surrounded by stunning medieval buildings adorned with colorful frescoes and intricate architecture. Be sure to visit the Torre dei Lamberti, a striking tower that stands at 84 meters tall. For a small fee of around $10, you can climb to the top for breathtaking panoramic views of the city.

To fully appreciate the atmosphere, grab a seat at one of the many outdoor cafes lining the square. Sip a cappuccino or indulge in a slice of authentic Italian pizza while enjoying the lively ambiance. The average price for a coffee is about $2, while a pizza can range from $10 to $15, depending on the toppings. Don't forget to try the local specialty, Pastissada de Cavalo, a horse meat stew that you can find at several restaurants nearby. The piazza is particularly lively in the evenings when street performers and musicians entertain crowds, making it a perfect spot for people-watching.

Just a short walk away is Piazza dei Signori, another picturesque square that exudes historical charm. This square features the impressive Statue of Dante, paying homage to the famed poet who spent time in Verona. The surrounding buildings showcase a mix of Gothic and Renaissance architecture, with elegant arches and intricate facades. Take the time to explore the shops that line the square, offering a variety of artisan goods, fashion, and souvenirs. Many shops sell handcrafted leather goods, jewelry, and local wines, allowing you to bring a piece of Verona home with you.

If you're visiting on a Sunday, the piazza hosts a charming antique market where you can find unique treasures and vintage items. Strolling through these lively squares, you'll find that each corner is alive with history, artistry, and the warmth of Italian culture. The combination of scenic views and delicious local food makes for an unforgettable experience in the heart of Verona.

Experience The Unique Blend Of Renaissance And Medieval Architecture Around Every Corner

Verona is a canvas painted with stunning architectural contrasts, where Renaissance elegance meets medieval robustness. As you wander through the city, you'll be captivated by the variety of styles that coexist harmoniously, showcasing Verona's rich history. Start your architectural exploration at the Piazza dei Signori, where the Palazzo della Ragione stands as a magnificent example of medieval architecture. This building, with its imposing facade and elegant arches, was once the seat of the city's government. Today, it hosts exhibitions and cultural events, making it a dynamic part of Verona's life.

One of the most striking features of Verona is the Castelvecchio, a medieval fortress that houses a museum of art and history. Its red brick walls and towering battlements provide a stark yet beautiful contrast to the surrounding Renaissance structures. The castle was built in the 14th century and is an excellent example of military architecture. For just $8, you can explore the museum's impressive collection of paintings, sculptures, and historical artifacts. The museum is open from 9 AM to 7 PM, and it's recommended to allow at least two hours to fully appreciate the exhibits.

As you stroll along the Ponte Scaligero, the bridge connecting Castelvecchio to the city, you'll be treated to stunning views of the Adige River and the surrounding hills. This bridge, with its iconic pointed arches, is a perfect spot for photographs. While the bridge is free to cross, you might want to stop at one of the riverside cafes to enjoy a refreshing drink while taking in the scenery. The average cost for a drink is around $4, making it an affordable way to soak up the local ambiance.

Another architectural marvel is the Basilica di San Zeno, known for its stunning Romanesque design. Located a bit away from the city center, this basilica is a must-see for architecture enthusiasts. The interior features beautiful frescoes and intricate woodwork, while the exterior is adorned with a magnificent rose window. The basilica is open from 10 AM to 12 PM and 3 PM to 5 PM, with a small admission fee of $6.

Exploring the unique blend of architectural styles in Verona is a feast for the eyes and soul. Whether you are gazing up at the intricate stonework of ancient buildings or marveling at the elegant lines of Renaissance palaces, every corner tells a story. The city's rich architectural tapestry provides a stunning backdrop for your adventures, making every moment spent here memorable.

Find Hidden Gems In The Cobblestone Alleyways That Tell Stories Of The Past

Beyond the well-trodden paths of Verona lie the enchanting cobblestone alleyways, each waiting to unveil its secrets. These narrow streets are steeped in history, filled with charming boutiques, local artisan shops, and authentic trattorias that serve up the best of Italian cuisine. As you wander through the labyrinth of alleys, you'll discover hidden gems that showcase the city's rich cultural heritage. One such treasure is Via Cappello, where you can find the entrance to Juliet's house, complete with her famous balcony. The alleyway leading to the house is lined with small shops selling love-themed souvenirs, making it a delightful experience for couples and romantics.

As you venture further, keep an eye out for the Palazzo Maffei, a hidden gem that features stunning baroque architecture. Its facade is adorned with statues and intricate carvings, showcasing the artistry of the era. Although it is often overshadowed by more famous landmarks, this palace is a fantastic photo opportunity. To enhance your experience, consider joining a walking tour that focuses on the lesser-known sites of Verona. These tours typically cost around $25 and provide insights into the city's hidden history, allowing you to discover stories and details that you might otherwise miss.

Another intriguing spot is Piazza della Pietra, a charming square featuring the remains of a Roman theatre. While it may not be as grand as the Verona Arena, this site holds its own historical significance. The area is often less crowded, making it a peaceful spot to rest and reflect. You can enjoy a coffee at a nearby café while taking in the surrounding architecture, which includes the remnants of ancient columns and arches. The average price for a coffee here is about $2, making it an affordable indulgence.

As the sun sets, the cobblestone alleys come alive with the glow of street lamps, casting a warm light on the historic buildings. This is the perfect time to explore the hidden taverns and wine bars that offer a taste of the local wine culture. Head to Enoteca Segreta, a cozy wine bar tucked away in the alleyways, where you can sample a selection of local wines paired with traditional snacks. A wine tasting experience here averages around $15 and is a delightful way to immerse yourself in the region's viticulture.

In the enchanting alleyways of Verona, every corner reveals a new story waiting to be discovered. From the vibrant cafes to the tranquil squares, these hidden gems provide a glimpse into the daily life of Veronese locals while allowing visitors to appreciate the city's rich history and charm. Embrace the adventure of wandering through these cobblestone streets, and you'll find that the true essence of Verona lies in the experiences waiting just off the main roads.

In summary, Verona offers a captivating blend of picturesque piazzas, stunning architectural styles, and charming hidden gems that make it a unique travel destination. Whether you're strolling through lively squares, marveling at the architectural contrasts, or exploring the enchanting alleyways, Verona invites you to immerse yourself in its rich history and vibrant culture. With each step, you'll uncover the stories that have shaped this beautiful city, ensuring your visit is both memorable and enriching.

CHAPTER 3:

INDULGE IN VERONA'S CULINARY DELIGHTS

Savor Local Dishes Like Risotto All'amarone And Pastissada De Caval

Verona's culinary scene is a delightful reflection of its rich history and local traditions, offering visitors a taste of authentic Italian cuisine. One of the must-try dishes is Risotto all'Amarone, a creamy rice dish made with the renowned Amarone wine, which is produced in the nearby Valpolicella region. This dish showcases the unique flavors of the area and is often served with seasonal vegetables or fresh herbs to enhance its taste. When ordering, you can expect to pay around $15 to $20 for a generous serving in most restaurants. For an unforgettable experience, consider dining at Trattoria al Pompiere, a beloved local eatery known for its warm ambiance and traditional dishes. It's advisable to make a reservation, especially during peak tourist seasons.

Another culinary delight that deserves a place on your plate is Pastissada de Caval, a hearty horse meat stew that has been a staple in Veronese cuisine for centuries. This dish is slow-cooked with a rich sauce of red wine, onions, and aromatic herbs, creating a deeply flavorful meal that embodies the essence of traditional cooking. You can find Pastissada de Caval on the menu at local trattorias, often served with polenta or fresh bread. The average price for this dish is about $18, making it a reasonably priced option for an authentic taste of Verona. For an authentic experience, head to Osteria Le Vecete, which offers a cozy atmosphere and a menu full of local specialties.

To truly savor the local cuisine, pair your meals with a glass of Valpolicella wine, known for its rich flavor and aromatic qualities. Local wineries often host tastings, providing an opportunity to learn more about the wine-making process and sample different varieties. A typical wine tasting experience costs around $25 and includes several tastings, along with expert guidance on food pairings. Many wineries in the Valpolicella region are easily accessible by public transport, making it convenient to incorporate into your culinary journey.

Discover The Vibrant Food Markets Where Fresh Produce And Local Specialties Abound

No visit to Verona would be complete without exploring its bustling food markets, where vibrant colors and enticing aromas create an unforgettable sensory experience. One of the most popular markets is the Piazza delle Erbe, which transforms into a lively market square every morning. Here, you'll find a delightful array of fresh produce, artisanal products, and local specialties. Vendors proudly showcase their goods, including ripe tomatoes, fragrant herbs, and a variety of cheeses and cured meats. It's a great opportunity to sample some local delicacies, often available for just a few dollars.

In addition to fresh fruits and vegetables, the market is also an excellent place to discover local specialties, such as Torta di Riso, a sweet rice cake that's a beloved treat in the region. Vendors often offer samples, allowing you to taste before you buy, and the average price for a slice is around $3. The market is open daily from 8 AM to 2 PM, but it's best to visit in the morning for the freshest selections.

Another gem to explore is the Mercato di Campagna Amica, located at Piazza San Zeno, which specializes in organic and locally sourced products. This market operates on Saturdays and features a range of vendors selling everything from fresh fruits and vegetables to homemade jams and artisan bread. The atmosphere is lively, and you'll often encounter local farmers and producers eager to share their stories and recommendations. A visit here allows you to connect with the local community while supporting sustainable practices.

When visiting these markets, consider bringing a reusable shopping bag to carry your purchases, as many vendors offer eco-friendly options. If you're looking for a unique souvenir, keep an eye out for local olive oils and balsamic vinegar, which make excellent gifts and are typically priced between $10 and $30, depending on the quality and quantity. Exploring these vibrant markets not only allows you to sample fresh, local produce but also immerses you in the heart of Veronese culture.

Join A Cooking Class To Learn How To Prepare Traditional Veronese Cuisine

To take your culinary experience in Verona to the next level, consider joining a cooking class that focuses on traditional Veronese cuisine. These classes offer a hands-on opportunity to learn from local chefs, who are eager to share their knowledge and passion for cooking. Many cooking schools, such as Cucina di Giuseppina, provide classes that include market visits, where you can hand-pick fresh ingredients before preparing a delicious meal together. The classes typically last around three hours and cost between $80 and $120 per person, depending on the menu and materials included.

During the class, you'll have the chance to learn how to prepare iconic dishes like Risotto all'Amarone or Pasta al Sugo d'Anatra (duck sauce pasta). These classes not only teach you essential cooking techniques but also the cultural significance behind each dish, making for a richer culinary experience. At the end of the session, you'll enjoy the fruits of your labor, dining on the delicious meal you've prepared alongside your fellow participants.

Many cooking classes also offer wine pairing suggestions, allowing you to appreciate the harmonious relationship between food and wine. This interactive experience creates lasting memories, and you'll leave with recipes and newfound skills to impress your friends and family back home.

Whether you're a seasoned cook or a beginner, joining a cooking class in Verona provides an authentic and immersive way to connect with the local culture. The combination of hands-on learning and delicious food makes it a highlight of any trip, ensuring you leave Verona not only with unforgettable memories but also with the ability to recreate a taste of Italy in your own kitchen.

In conclusion, Verona's culinary scene is rich with flavors and traditions that are waiting to be discovered. From savoring local dishes like Risotto all'Amarone and Pastissada de Caval to exploring vibrant food markets and participating in cooking classes, there's no shortage of delicious experiences to enjoy. Each step you take in this charming city brings you closer to its culinary heart, ensuring your visit is filled with unforgettable tastes and stories. As you explore Verona's food culture, you'll find that every meal is not just about nourishment but a celebration of tradition, community, and the love of good food.

CHAPTER 4:

EXPERIENCE THE CULTURE AND ARTS SCENE

Attend A Performance At The Iconic Verona Arena, Especially During The Summer Opera Season

One of the highlights of any visit to Verona is attending a performance at the Verona Arena, a remarkable Roman amphitheater that has stood the test of time. Dating back to 30 AD, this architectural marvel is renowned for its impressive acoustics and stunning atmosphere, making it one of the premier venues for opera performances in the world. The summer opera season typically runs from June to September, featuring classic productions such as Aida, La Traviata, and Carmen. Prices for tickets can vary widely based on the seat location, ranging from $25 in the upper tiers to over $200 for prime seats in the lower sections. Booking in advance is highly recommended, as performances often sell out quickly.

When planning your visit, consider arriving early to enjoy a pre-show aperitivo in one of the nearby piazzas. The lively atmosphere of Verona in the summer adds to the magic of the evening, with locals and tourists alike mingling in the warm glow of the setting sun. The Arena opens approximately two hours before the show starts, allowing you ample time to explore the exterior and soak in the historical significance of this iconic landmark. Additionally, it's a good idea to dress comfortably, as evenings can get cool, especially after the sun sets.

For a truly unforgettable experience, consider opting for a VIP package that includes a guided tour of the Arena and a gourmet dinner at a nearby restaurant. This package usually ranges from $150 to $300 per person and provides an insider's view of the Arena's history and architecture. As the evening draws to a close, the powerful performances and the breathtaking backdrop of the ancient structure will leave you with lasting memories of Verona's vibrant cultural scene.

Explore The Art Galleries And Museums Showcasing Local And International Artists

Verona is not only famous for its historical sites and opera performances but also boasts a thriving art scene that is worth exploring. The city's art galleries and museums offer a glimpse into both local talent and international artistry, providing a rich cultural experience. A must-visit is the Museo di Castelvecchio, housed in a stunning medieval castle. This museum features an impressive collection of paintings, sculptures, and artifacts from the Middle Ages to the Renaissance. Admission is around $10, and the museum is open Tuesday through Sunday from 8:30 AM to 7:30 PM. Don't miss the chance to walk along the museum's walls, where you can enjoy breathtaking views of the Adige River and the surrounding city.

In addition to Castelvecchio, Galleria d'Arte Moderna Palazzo Forti is another highlight. This gallery showcases 19th- and 20th-century Italian art and hosts temporary exhibitions featuring contemporary artists. The entrance fee is approximately $8, and the gallery is open Wednesday to Sunday, from 10 AM to 7 PM. The unique blend of historical and modern art provides a comprehensive view of Verona's artistic evolution.

For those who enjoy street art, exploring the city's urban landscape reveals vibrant murals and installations that reflect the contemporary art scene. The Murales di Verona project has transformed various neighborhoods, allowing visitors to appreciate art in unexpected places. Be sure to take your time wandering through these areas, camera in hand, to capture the striking artwork.

To get the most out of your art exploration, consider joining a guided walking tour that focuses on Verona's artistic heritage. These tours typically last around two hours and cost about $25 per person. Knowledgeable local guides will share fascinating insights about the artists and their works, enriching your understanding of Verona's art scene.

Visit The Annual Verona Jazz Festival To Enjoy Live Music In A Beautiful Setting

For music enthusiasts, the Verona Jazz Festival is a highlight of the city's cultural calendar. Held annually in late July, this festival draws talented musicians from around the globe to perform in various stunning venues throughout the city, including historic piazzas and scenic parks. The festival typically features a diverse lineup, from jazz legends to emerging artists, offering something for everyone. Ticket prices vary depending on the venue and artist, but expect to pay around $20 to $50 for a general admission ticket to most performances.

Attending the Verona Jazz Festival is a unique way to experience the city's vibrant atmosphere while enjoying high-quality live music. The festival not only showcases individual performances but often includes collaborative jam sessions and workshops, making it an engaging event for both musicians and fans alike. Be sure to check the festival's official website for the complete lineup and schedule, as well as any special events or ticketing information.

One of the best aspects of the Verona Jazz Festival is the opportunity to enjoy performances in picturesque settings, such as the Giardini dell'Arena, a beautiful garden area adjacent to the Verona Arena. This setting allows you to sip local wines or enjoy food from nearby vendors while soaking up the sounds of talented musicians. As the sun sets, the ambiance transforms, making for a memorable evening under the stars.

To enhance your festival experience, consider arriving early to explore the local food scene or participating in pre-show events, such as open mic nights or music workshops. Engaging with fellow music lovers and artists will enrich your understanding of the local jazz culture and may even lead to new friendships.

In conclusion, Verona offers a rich tapestry of cultural experiences that extend beyond its historical landmarks. Attending a performance at the Verona Arena, exploring local art galleries, and enjoying the vibrant atmosphere of the Verona Jazz Festival are just a few ways to immerse yourself in the city's artistic and musical heritage. Each experience provides a unique insight into Verona's cultural fabric, ensuring your visit is filled with memorable moments and lasting impressions. Whether you're an opera aficionado, an art enthusiast, or a jazz lover, Verona's cultural scene promises to captivate and inspire you during your journey through this enchanting Italian city.

CHAPTER 5:

UNWIND IN VERONA'S SCENIC PARKS AND GARDENS

Relax In The Lush Giardino Giusti, A Perfect Spot For A Peaceful Retreat

Nestled in the heart of Verona, Giardino Giusti is a stunning Renaissance garden that provides a serene escape from the bustling city. Created in the 16th century by the noble Giusti family, this beautifully landscaped garden is adorned with a variety of trees, hedges, and fountains, making it an ideal spot for relaxation and contemplation. The entrance fee is approximately $6, and the garden is open from 8 AM to 7:30 PM during the summer months, allowing ample time to explore its lush surroundings.

As you stroll along the winding paths, you'll encounter meticulously designed flower beds and classical sculptures that offer a glimpse into the opulent lifestyle of its former inhabitants. The garden features terraced lawns that ascend towards the hilltop, providing visitors with breathtaking views of the city skyline and the distant hills. A highlight of your visit will undoubtedly be the spectacular panoramic view from the top terrace, where you can capture unforgettable photos of Verona's rooftops and the Adige River snaking through the city.

For those seeking a peaceful retreat, Giardino Giusti is also a fantastic place to simply unwind. Bring along a book or a sketch pad and find a quiet bench amidst the greenery. The gentle rustling of leaves and the distant sound of birds chirping create a tranquil atmosphere, perfect for recharging after a busy day of sightseeing. Additionally, the garden often hosts cultural events and art exhibitions, so check their official website for any scheduled activities during your visit.

If you're feeling peckish, you can find a small café at the entrance that serves light snacks and refreshments. A leisurely afternoon spent in Giardino Giusti is a wonderful way to escape the crowds and connect with nature while experiencing one of Verona's hidden gems.

Take In Breathtaking Views Of The City From The Castel San Pietro

For those who appreciate stunning vistas, Castel San Pietro offers one of the best viewpoints in Verona. Perched atop a hill overlooking the city, this historic fortress dates back to the 14th century and provides a fascinating glimpse into Verona's military past. The castle is open to the public and is free to enter, although there may be a small fee for guided tours if you wish to delve deeper into its history.

Reaching Castel San Pietro requires a bit of a climb, but the journey is well worth it. You can either hike up the winding paths that lead to the fortress or take the convenient funicular railway, which operates daily from 7:30 AM to 9 PM for about $2. The funicular ride itself is an enjoyable experience, as it ascends smoothly while offering increasingly impressive views of the city below.

Once you arrive at the castle, take a moment to explore the ruins and appreciate the intricate architecture of this ancient structure.

From the castle's ramparts, you'll be treated to panoramic views of Verona, including the majestic Ponte Pietra, the Adige River, and the iconic Verona Arena in the distance. As the sun begins to set, the golden hues of the sky cast a magical glow over the city, making it an unforgettable moment for visitors and photographers alike.

To enhance your visit, consider packing a picnic to enjoy on the castle grounds. There are several benches and grassy areas where you can relax while taking in the breathtaking scenery. Whether you choose to visit during the day to explore the historical significance of the fortress or in the evening to witness the stunning sunset, Castel San Pietro is a must-see for anyone seeking an extraordinary perspective of Verona.

Discover The Botanical Beauty Of The Parco Dell'adige, Perfect For A Leisurely Walk

The Parco dell'Adige is a delightful urban park that runs alongside the river, offering a peaceful setting for leisurely strolls and outdoor activities. Spanning approximately 18 kilometers, this park provides a green oasis in the heart of Verona, making it an ideal escape for nature lovers and families alike. Admission to the park is free, and it's open year-round, allowing visitors to enjoy its beauty in all seasons.

As you wander through the park, you'll encounter a variety of native plants and trees, as well as well-maintained walking and cycling paths that wind along the riverbank. The gentle sounds of the flowing water and the rustling leaves create a calming atmosphere, perfect for unwinding after a day of exploring the city's historical sites. Keep your eyes peeled for the diverse birdlife that inhabits the area, including ducks, herons, and various songbirds.

One of the highlights of the Parco dell'Adige is the opportunity to discover several picturesque spots along the river. Take a moment to relax on one of the benches by the water or bring a blanket for a picnic amidst the lush greenery. Additionally, the park features various playgrounds for children, making it a family-friendly destination.

If you're interested in cycling, consider renting a bike to explore more of the park and its surroundings. There are several rental shops in the city center, with prices starting at around $10 for a half-day rental. Biking along the river is a wonderful way to take in the scenic views and enjoy the fresh air.

For those who enjoy a more structured experience, guided walking tours of the park are also available, often focusing on the flora and fauna native to the region. These tours typically cost around $15 per person and provide fascinating insights into the park's ecological significance.

In summary, Verona's outdoor spaces, including Giardino Giusti, Castel San Pietro, and Parco dell'Adige, offer visitors a chance to connect with nature and enjoy the city's natural beauty. Each location provides a unique perspective of Verona, allowing for peaceful retreats, breathtaking views, and leisurely walks amidst the botanical splendor.

Whether you're looking to relax, explore, or simply take a moment to appreciate the serenity of the great outdoors, these parks are essential stops on your Verona itinerary.

CHAPTER 6:

SHOP LIKE A LOCAL IN VERONA

Browse Through Boutique Shops Offering Unique Italian Fashion And Artisanal Goods

Exploring Verona's vibrant shopping scene is an essential part of any visit, and the city's boutique shops offer a delightful blend of unique Italian fashion and artisanal goods. Strolling through these charming streets, visitors will discover a plethora of shops that showcase the creativity and craftsmanship of local artisans. The atmosphere is imbued with the rich history and culture of the city, making shopping not just an errand but a memorable experience.

One of the best areas to start your shopping adventure is the Via Mazzini, a bustling pedestrian street lined with an array of boutiques, from high-end fashion to quaint artisanal shops. Here, you can find unique clothing items that reflect the latest Italian trends, with styles ranging from chic modern designs to classic vintage pieces. Expect to pay around $100 to $300 for a quality designer outfit, depending on the brand and materials used. This street is also home to famous Italian labels like Gucci and Prada, alongside lesser-known but equally stylish boutiques.

For those in search of artisanal goods, the nearby Piazza delle Erbe is a treasure trove. This historic marketplace has existed since the Roman era and continues to thrive as a hub for local artisans. Vendors set up stalls selling everything from handcrafted leather goods and handmade jewelry to beautiful ceramics and textiles. A unique leather handbag can be found here for about $60 to $150, while artisan jewelry typically ranges from $20 to $100, making it easy to find a special souvenir that embodies the spirit of Verona.

The artisans in these shops take pride in their craft, often welcoming visitors to witness the creation of their products firsthand. For instance, at Bottega del Vino, not only can you purchase exquisite wine from the surrounding region, but you can also explore a curated selection of wine-related accessories, such as hand-blown glass decanters and handcrafted corkscrews. These items, typically priced between $30 and $150, make for thoughtful gifts that showcase the essence of Veronese culture.

To get the most out of your shopping experience, be sure to visit during the weekdays when the shops are less crowded, allowing for a more leisurely pace as you explore. Engaging with shopkeepers and artisans can also enhance your experience, as they are often eager to share stories about their work and the inspiration behind their creations. Many shops offer discounts for cash payments, so it's worthwhile to have some euros on hand.

Additionally, Verona hosts various seasonal markets and craft fairs throughout the year, showcasing the talents of local artisans. Events like the Verona Christmas Market attract visitors from all over, offering an expanded selection of handmade goods and festive treats. If your visit coincides with such events, make sure to include them in your itinerary for an authentic shopping experience.

Explore The Local Markets For Handmade Crafts And Delicious Local Products

Beyond the boutique shops, the local markets of Verona are an integral part of the city's cultural fabric, showcasing the craftsmanship and culinary delights of the region. Piazza delle Erbe transforms into a vibrant market during the daytime, where local vendors gather to sell their handmade crafts and delicious local products. The market is typically open from 8 AM to 1 PM daily, offering a lively atmosphere filled with the sounds and scents of Italy.

In this marketplace, you'll find an assortment of handmade crafts that reflect the city's artistic heritage. From intricately designed pottery to beautifully woven textiles, the quality and craftsmanship are unparalleled. Local artisans take great pride in their work, ensuring that each piece tells a story.

Handmade ceramics, for example, can range from $15 to $50, making them a perfect gift or keepsake.

One of the standout features of the market is its selection of delicious local products. Visitors can sample a variety of cheeses, cured meats, and fresh produce. Don't miss the chance to taste Monte Veronese, a cheese produced in the nearby mountains, known for its rich flavor and crumbly texture. A good wedge typically costs around $10. You can also find delectable Salame di Verona, a locally made salami that pairs beautifully with the region's artisanal cheeses.

For those interested in more than just browsing, many vendors offer cooking demonstrations or tastings. This is an excellent opportunity to learn about the traditional methods of food preparation and to gain insight into the local culinary scene. Be sure to ask vendors about their specialties; they often have tips on how to incorporate their products into your meals back home.

The local markets also host a range of seasonal products, making each visit unique. In the fall, for example, you might find an abundance of mushrooms and truffles, while spring brings fresh asparagus and artichokes. The changing seasons provide a delightful way to experience the region's agricultural bounty.

In addition to Piazza delle Erbe, consider visiting Mercato di Piazza San Zeno, held on Saturdays from 8 AM to 1 PM. This market is smaller but just as charming, featuring local produce, meats, and a range of handmade goods. Engaging with local farmers and artisans here provides a more intimate shopping experience. The prices are often more reasonable than in shops, making it a fantastic way to sample authentic Veronese products without breaking the bank.

Learn About The City's Shopping Districts, From Luxury Brands To Traditional Artisans

Verona is home to various shopping districts, each offering a distinct experience that caters to different tastes and budgets. From luxury brands to traditional artisans, you can find everything your heart desires while exploring the city's enchanting streets.

Start your shopping journey in the Centro Storico, Verona's historic center, where you'll find a blend of high-end fashion boutiques and traditional shops. Here, the atmosphere is imbued with history, and as you wander through the cobblestone streets, you'll pass by iconic landmarks such as the Arena di Verona and Piazza dei Signori. This area is perfect for a leisurely shopping spree, with designer boutiques like Dolce & Gabbana and Fendi situated alongside family-owned shops selling artisanal goods.

For those looking to indulge in luxury shopping, Via Mazzini is the main thoroughfare, lined with international fashion brands and upscale boutiques. You can easily spend an afternoon browsing the stylish storefronts, and prices will vary widely, with luxury items starting at around $200. It's also common to find sales, particularly during the summer and winter months, so keep an eye out for deals if you're looking to splurge.

If you prefer a more local experience, head to the Porta Borsari area, known for its traditional artisan shops. Here, you can find skilled craftspeople who create everything from handmade leather goods to intricate lacework. Visit Pellegrini Leather Goods for beautifully crafted bags and wallets, where prices typically range from $50 to $300, depending on the item. The quality of these handmade goods far surpasses that of mass-produced items, making them well worth the investment.

Don't miss the opportunity to explore the Vicolo Santa Lucia, a charming narrow street filled with workshops and shops run by artisans who have passed down their skills through generations. This area is especially famous for its mosaic tiles and handmade jewelry. The artisans here often welcome visitors into their studios, offering a glimpse into their creative process and the chance to purchase unique pieces that you won't find elsewhere. Prices for artisan jewelry start around $20, while more elaborate pieces can cost upwards of $150.

To maximize your shopping experience, consider visiting during the weekdays when shops are less crowded. Many boutique owners are more than happy to engage with customers and share their stories. This personal touch enhances the shopping experience, allowing you to connect with the local culture on a deeper level.

As you explore Verona's shopping districts, be sure to take breaks at one of the many cafés or gelaterias that dot the streets. Enjoying a delicious gelato or a cappuccino not only gives you a chance to rest but also lets you soak in the local ambiance. Don't forget to indulge in the local delicacies; a scoop of gelato typically costs around $3, while a coffee will set you back about $2.

In conclusion, Verona offers a diverse and enchanting shopping experience that combines luxury fashion with traditional artisanal goods. Whether you're strolling through the boutiques on Via Mazzini or exploring the vibrant local markets, you'll find something special that reflects the city's rich heritage. Embrace the opportunity to connect with local artisans, discover unique products, and create lasting memories during your shopping adventure in Verona.

CHAPTER 7:

IMMERSE YOURSELF IN VERONA'S FESTIVALS

Join The Lively Carnival Celebrations That Bring The City To Life With Colorful Parades

Verona's Carnival celebrations are a spectacular display of color, culture, and tradition that captivates both locals and visitors alike. Held annually in February, the festivities transform the city into a vibrant playground filled with lively parades, masks, music, and dancing. The origins of the Verona Carnival can be traced back to the 13th century, making it a cherished event that showcases the rich heritage of the city.

As the celebration kicks off, the streets become alive with a variety of events and activities. The main highlight is undoubtedly the grand parade, which features elaborate floats, colorful costumes, and enthusiastic performers. Each year, different themes are chosen, allowing for creativity and innovation in the designs. Participants, dressed in stunning masks and costumes, take to the streets to celebrate the spirit of Carnival, creating a mesmerizing visual feast that enchants everyone who witnesses it. Expect to see vibrant displays that reflect both traditional Italian culture and contemporary artistry.

To make the most of your Carnival experience, arrive early to secure a good viewing spot along the parade route. The main parade typically occurs on the last Sunday before Lent, but other festivities often take place throughout the week leading up to the main event. Make sure to check the official Carnival schedule, which is usually available online a few weeks prior to the celebrations, detailing times and locations of various activities. The festivities kick off in the Piazza Bra, near the iconic Arena, and wind through the city, creating an immersive experience that allows visitors to explore Verona's charming streets.

During the celebrations, you'll find numerous food stalls offering traditional Carnival treats such as chiacchiere, sweet fried pastries dusted with powdered sugar, and frittelle, delicious sweet fritters often filled with cream or fruit. These treats typically cost between $2 to $5, making them a perfect snack as you take in the sights and sounds of the parade. Local bars and cafés also join in on the festivities, offering special drinks and treats that celebrate the spirit of Carnival.

While the parades are undoubtedly the main attraction, there are plenty of other activities to enjoy throughout the week. Families can participate in various workshops where they can learn about traditional mask-making, allowing them to create their own unique piece to wear during the celebrations. These workshops can range from $10 to $30, depending on the materials used.

As evening falls, the celebrations continue with live music, street performers, and dances in various squares throughout the city. Be sure to join in the festivities and dance the night away, experiencing the true essence of Carnival in Verona. With its historical significance, colorful parades, and festive atmosphere, joining the Carnival celebrations is a must for anyone visiting the city in February.

Experience The Annual Vinitaly Wine Fair, A Must For Wine Lovers And Connoisseurs

For wine enthusiasts, the annual VinItaly wine fair is an event not to be missed. Taking place in April at the Verona Exhibition Centre, VinItaly is one of the largest and most prestigious wine fairs in the world. This remarkable event attracts wine producers, distributors, and connoisseurs from around the globe, making it a hub for networking, tasting, and learning about the latest trends in the wine industry.

The fair typically spans four days and features thousands of exhibitors showcasing their finest wines. This includes an impressive array of Italian wines from various regions, including renowned names like Barolo, Brunello di Montalcino, and of course, the famous Amarone della Valpolicella. Each year, attendees have the opportunity to taste thousands of wines, attend educational seminars, and participate in masterclasses led by industry experts. Ticket prices for the event generally range from $30 to $50, with options for early bird purchases available online.

To get the most out of your VinItaly experience, plan your visit ahead of time. It's a good idea to check the official website for schedules of tastings, workshops, and seminars. Early registration allows you to secure spots in popular masterclasses, where you can delve deeper into the nuances of winemaking and tasting techniques. These classes are typically priced between $50 to $150, depending on the level of expertise and the wines featured.

Navigating the exhibition center can be overwhelming due to the sheer number of exhibitors and activities, so it's wise to grab a map and mark the booths of the wineries you're most interested in. Don't hesitate to engage with the producers; they are often passionate about their wines and eager to share their knowledge. Sampling local specialties like cheeses, cured meats, and olive oils at various stalls is also a highlight of the fair.

In addition to the tasting opportunities, VinItaly also hosts several awards ceremonies that celebrate outstanding wines. The Vinitaly Wine Competition recognizes excellence in the industry, highlighting wines that stand out for their quality and craftsmanship. This is a fantastic opportunity for attendees to discover new favorites and trends in the wine market.

Attending VinItaly not only allows you to indulge in the world of fine wines but also connects you with a community of like-minded individuals who share a passion for oenology. Whether you are a casual wine drinker or a serious connoisseur, this event is sure to enrich your appreciation for Italian wines and the artistry behind them.

Discover The Local Traditions During The Feast Of St. Anastasia In April

April is a particularly lively month in Verona, marked by the celebration of the Feast of St. Anastasia. This local festival, held on April 16th, is dedicated to the patron saint of Verona and features a blend of religious and cultural traditions that showcase the city's deep-rooted heritage. St. Anastasia, a significant figure in the history of Verona, is celebrated through various ceremonies, processions, and community activities that bring together locals and visitors alike.

The festivities kick off with a solemn mass held in the Basilica di San Zeno, one of the city's most beautiful churches. The basilica, a UNESCO World Heritage site, is renowned for its stunning architecture and rich history. Attending the mass is a meaningful way to connect with the local community and experience the spiritual significance of the feast. The service typically starts around 10 AM, and it's advisable to arrive early to secure a good spot, as the basilica often fills up quickly during this popular event.

Following the mass, the atmosphere shifts to a more festive spirit with a vibrant procession through the city streets. Participants dressed in traditional costumes carry the statue of St. Anastasia, accompanied by music and dancing. The procession winds its way through the historical center, with locals and visitors lining the streets to join in the celebrations. This lively display of faith and community spirit creates an unforgettable experience, showcasing the warmth and hospitality of the Veronese people.

Throughout the day, various cultural events and activities take place across the city. Local artisans and craftsmen often set up stalls in the Piazza delle Erbe, showcasing their handmade products and traditional crafts. This is a great opportunity to purchase unique souvenirs that reflect the culture of Verona. Prices for handmade goods can range from $10 to $100, depending on the item.

Food also plays a significant role in the Feast of St. Anastasia. Traditional dishes are prepared and served at local restaurants and food stalls, allowing visitors to savor authentic

Veronese cuisine. You might encounter dishes like Risotto all'Amarone, a creamy rice dish made with the region's famous red wine, or Pastissada de Caval, a hearty horse meat stew that is a local specialty. Expect to pay around $15 to $30 for a meal at a local trattoria, where you can immerse yourself in the flavors of the region while enjoying the lively atmosphere.

To enhance your experience of the Feast of St. Anastasia, consider participating in some of the cultural workshops that are often offered during the festival. These workshops may include traditional music, dance, and cooking classes, providing a hands-on way to engage with Veronese culture. Prices for these activities vary but generally range from $20 to $50, depending on the duration and materials included.

In conclusion, joining the lively Carnival celebrations, experiencing the renowned VinItaly wine fair, and discovering the local traditions during the Feast of St. Anastasia all offer unique glimpses into the vibrant culture of Verona. Each of these events not only highlights the city's rich history and community spirit but also provides opportunities for visitors to engage with local traditions and enjoy the flavors of the region. Whether you are dancing in the streets during Carnival, sipping exquisite wines at VinItaly, or partaking in the heartfelt celebrations of St. Anastasia, your visit to Verona will be filled with unforgettable experiences and lasting memories.

CHAPTER 8:

EXPLORE THE SURROUNDING COUNTRYSIDE

Venture Into The Stunning Valpolicella Region, Known For Its Exquisite Wines

Just a stone's throw from Verona lies the breathtaking Valpolicella region, a picturesque area renowned for its exquisite wines, particularly Amarone della Valpolicella. This enchanting landscape is characterized by rolling hills, lush vineyards, and charming villages, making it a must-visit for wine lovers and nature enthusiasts alike. Valpolicella is steeped in a rich winemaking tradition that dates back thousands of years, and the region's unique climate and soil conditions create the perfect environment for cultivating high-quality grapes.

The primary grape varieties grown in Valpolicella are Corvina, Molinara, and Rondinella, which are blended to create the region's signature wines. A visit to one of the many wineries in the area offers a delightful opportunity to taste these exceptional wines, learn about the winemaking process, and understand the local culture that surrounds it. Many wineries offer guided tours and tastings, where you can sample various vintages and even pair them with local culinary delights. Prices for these experiences typically range from $15 to $50 per person, depending on the winery and the number of wines sampled.

One of the most celebrated wineries in Valpolicella is Tommasi Viticoltori, located in the heart of the region. Here, visitors can take a guided tour of the vineyard, learn about the traditional appassimento process used to make Amarone, and taste a selection of wines accompanied by local cheeses and cured meats. The winery's address is Via G. Tommasi 7, 37029 Pedemonte VR, Italy. They can be reached at +39 045 686 1296, and reservations are recommended, especially during peak tourist seasons.

To enhance your experience in Valpolicella, consider visiting during the grape harvest season, typically in late September to early October. This is a bustling time in the region, with many wineries hosting special events and activities, allowing visitors to participate in the harvest and experience the joy of winemaking firsthand.

In addition to its renowned wines, Valpolicella offers stunning natural beauty, with numerous hiking and cycling trails that wind through the vineyards and olive groves. For a truly unforgettable experience, plan a picnic among the vines, where you can enjoy a bottle of local wine while soaking in the picturesque surroundings.

Visit The Charming Nearby Towns Of Lake Garda For Beautiful Lakeside Views

A short drive from Verona leads you to the enchanting shores of Lake Garda, Italy's largest lake, where charming towns and stunning lakeside views await. The region is known for its breathtaking landscapes, crystal-clear waters, and picturesque towns, each offering its own unique charm and attractions. Whether you're looking to relax by the water, explore quaint streets, or enjoy outdoor activities, Lake Garda has something for everyone.

One of the most popular towns along the lake is Sirmione, famous for its thermal baths, historical sites, and stunning waterfront views. The Scaliger Castle, a 13th-century fortress, dominates the town's skyline and provides a fascinating glimpse into the area's history. Visitors can wander through the narrow cobblestone streets, lined with shops and restaurants, and sample local delicacies. A visit to Sirmione isn't complete without trying the region's signature dish, bigoli con le sarde, a pasta dish with sardines, which typically costs around $12 to $20 at local trattorias.

To reach Sirmione from Verona, you can take a train to Desenzano del Garda (about 30 minutes) and then a bus or ferry to Sirmione. Alternatively, driving takes about 40 minutes, offering beautiful scenic views along the way. Parking can be limited in Sirmione, especially during peak tourist seasons, so it's best to arrive early.

Another charming town to explore is Riva del Garda, located at the northern end of the lake. Surrounded by dramatic mountains, Riva del Garda is a paradise for outdoor enthusiasts, offering opportunities for hiking, biking, and water sports. The Piazza 3 Novembre is a lovely spot to relax, with stunning views of the lake and the ancient Torre Apponale clock tower. After exploring, indulge in a gelato from one of the many gelaterias in the area, with prices ranging from $2 to $5.

For those seeking a more tranquil experience, Garda and Bardolino are beautiful towns located along the eastern shore of the lake. Garda offers a charming lakeside promenade, perfect for leisurely strolls, while Bardolino is renowned for its excellent wines, particularly the light, fruity Bardolino rosé. Wineries in this area often provide tours and tastings, allowing visitors to experience the local wine culture firsthand.

(Lake Garda's stunning scenery makes it a prime location for outdoor activities. Renting a boat or taking a guided boat tour of the lake is a fantastic way to appreciate its beauty from the water. Prices for boat rentals typically start around $30 for an hour, while guided tours can range from $25 to $60 per person, depending on the duration and inclusions.)

A visit to Lake Garda offers a delightful combination of relaxation, culture, and outdoor adventure. The charming towns along its shores, with their beautiful lakeside views and rich history, make for an unforgettable day trip from Verona.

Experience The Breathtaking Scenery Of The Lessinia Natural Park

For those looking to immerse themselves in nature, a visit to Lessinia Natural Park is a must. Located just north of Verona, this expansive park encompasses over 10,000 hectares of stunning landscapes, including mountains, valleys, and lush forests. Lessinia is known for its breathtaking scenery, rich biodiversity, and numerous outdoor activities, making it an ideal destination for hiking, wildlife watching, and exploring the natural beauty of the Italian countryside.

The park is home to various hiking trails suitable for all levels, ranging from easy strolls to challenging treks. One of the most popular routes is the Strada delle 52 Gallerie, a historic military road that features 52 tunnels and offers spectacular views of the surrounding mountains and valleys. This hike typically takes about four to six hours to complete, depending on your pace, and is approximately 10 kilometers (6 miles) in length. Make sure to wear sturdy hiking boots and bring plenty of water and snacks, as there are limited facilities along the trail.

Lessinia is also famous for its rich flora and fauna, including rare species of plants, birds, and other wildlife. Keep your eyes peeled for local wildlife, such as deer, foxes, and various bird species, as you explore the park. The park's visitor centers often provide guided nature walks, which can enhance your experience by offering insights into the local ecosystem and geology. Prices for guided tours usually range from $15 to $30 per person.

Another notable feature of Lessinia is its traditional stone houses, known as malghe, which were used by farmers during the summer months. These charming structures dot the landscape and serve as a reminder of the region's agricultural heritage. Many malghe have been restored and now offer opportunities to taste local cheeses, such as Monte Veronese, made from the milk of local cows and goats. Sampling these cheeses is a delightful way to experience the flavors of the region, with prices typically ranging from $5 to $15 for a tasting platter.

If you're visiting in the summer, consider attending one of the many local festivals celebrating the region's traditions, such as the Festa del Formaggio (Cheese Festival), where you can sample various cheeses and enjoy local music and entertainment. This festival usually takes place in late July and provides a fantastic opportunity to experience the local culture while savoring delicious food.

In conclusion, venturing into the stunning Valpolicella region, visiting the charming towns of Lake Garda, and experiencing the breathtaking scenery of the Lessinia Natural Park all offer unique and enriching experiences that showcase the diverse beauty of the Verona area. Whether you're indulging in exquisite wines, taking in beautiful lakeside views, or exploring the natural wonders of the park, these adventures will leave you with lasting memories and a deeper appreciation for this captivating part of Italy. Each of these destinations not only highlights the rich cultural heritage and natural beauty of the region but also provides opportunities to connect with the local community and savor the flavors of Northern Italy.

CHAPTER 9:

DELVE INTO VERONA'S WINE CULTURE

Tour Local Vineyards To Taste The Famous Amarone And Valpolicella Wines

Exploring the local vineyards of the Valpolicella region is a delightful journey into the heart of Italy's wine country, renowned for its exceptional wines, particularly Amarone della Valpolicella and Valpolicella Classico. Nestled just a short drive from Verona, this enchanting area features rolling hills, charming wineries, and picturesque vineyards, making it a paradise for wine lovers. A visit to Valpolicella offers an immersive experience where you can savor the rich flavors of the region while soaking in the breathtaking scenery.

Start your wine adventure at Cantina di Negrar, one of the oldest wineries in the region, established in 1933. The winery is known for its commitment to quality and tradition, producing some of the best Amarone and Valpolicella wines. During your visit, you can participate in guided tours that take you through the vineyard, showcasing the traditional grape varieties used in their wines, such as Corvina, Rondinella, and Molinara. Tours typically last about 1.5 hours and include tastings of several wines, allowing you to experience the unique characteristics of each. The cost for a tasting experience usually ranges from $15 to $40 per person, depending on the number of wines sampled and whether you choose to pair them with local cheeses or cured meats.

Cantina di Negrar is located at Via della Casetta 14, 37024 Negrar di Valpolicella VR, Italy, and you can reach them at +39 045 601 8100. It is advisable to book your visit in advance, especially during peak tourist seasons. This winery provides an excellent introduction to the region's winemaking heritage, and you'll leave with a greater appreciation for the complexities of Amarone, a rich, full-bodied wine made from partially dried grapes.

Another fantastic option is Villa Mosconi, a family-run vineyard that offers an authentic experience of Valpolicella winemaking. The estate's vineyards are beautifully maintained, and the owners are passionate about sharing their knowledge of wine production. Here, you can enjoy a tasting of their award-winning Amarone and Valpolicella wines in a charming setting. Villa Mosconi is located at Via Cà Bassa, 7, 37029, San Pietro in Cariano VR, Italy. You can call them at +39 045 600 4535 for reservations.

Visiting these vineyards offers an opportunity to learn firsthand about the winemaking process. Most wineries provide insights into the traditional methods of grape harvesting, fermentation, and aging that contribute to the unique flavor profiles of the wines. The process of making Amarone, for example, involves drying the harvested grapes for several months before fermentation, which concentrates their sugars and flavors, resulting in a rich, complex wine.

(Learn more about the region's rich viticulture history during your visits, as many wineries display historical artifacts, vintage wine bottles, and photographs that illustrate the evolution of winemaking in Valpolicella. This journey through time allows you to appreciate the passion and dedication that has gone into crafting these exceptional wines for generations.)

Learn About The Winemaking Process And The Region's Rich Viticulture History

Valpolicella's history of winemaking stretches back to ancient Roman times, making it one of the oldest wine regions in Italy. The name "Valpolicella" itself is derived from the Latin word "Vallis Pulli Cellae," meaning "valley of many cellars." The region has long been celebrated for its fertile soil, favorable climate, and unique grape varieties, which have contributed to its reputation as a premier winemaking destination.

A key aspect of the winemaking process in Valpolicella is the appassimento technique, which is used to create Amarone. After harvesting, the grapes are laid out on wooden racks to dry for several months, allowing them to lose moisture and concentrate their sugars. This method, combined with the region's diverse terroir, results in a wine that is rich in flavor, with notes of dried fruit, chocolate, and spices.

During your vineyard tours, take advantage of the opportunity to learn about the various steps involved in the winemaking process. Many wineries offer workshops that delve into specific aspects of winemaking, from blending techniques to barrel aging. These hands-on experiences can deepen your understanding of how different factors influence the final product. Participating in a workshop typically costs around $30 to $70 per person, depending on the length and content of the session.

One notable workshop is offered by Corte Giara, where participants can learn about the entire winemaking process, from grape selection to bottling. They provide a unique opportunity to get involved in the winemaking process and taste wines that are still in development. The cost for this interactive experience is about $40 per person, which includes tastings of different wine stages.

The region's viticulture history is also celebrated through events and festivals dedicated to wine and food. The annual Vinitaly wine fair, held in April in Verona, attracts wine producers, distributors, and wine lovers from around the world. This event showcases the best wines from Italy and provides opportunities for tastings, workshops, and networking. Attending Vinitaly is an excellent way to immerse yourself in Italy's wine culture, with entry tickets typically priced around $30 to $50 for a day pass.

Additionally, many wineries in Valpolicella participate in Open Cellars, a nationwide event where vineyards welcome visitors for tastings, tours, and educational sessions about wine production. This event usually takes place in late May and is a fantastic opportunity to experience the region's winemaking firsthand while interacting with local producers. Many wineries also offer special discounts on wine purchases during this event, making it a great time to stock up on your favorite bottles.

Attend Wine Tastings And Workshops To Deepen Your Appreciation For Italian Wines

Attending wine tastings and workshops in Valpolicella is a must for anyone looking to deepen their appreciation for Italian wines. These experiences allow you to explore the nuances of different varietals and learn about the intricate details that go into each bottle. Many wineries in the region offer curated tasting experiences, showcasing their best wines and highlighting the unique characteristics of each.

One popular option is the Amarone Tasting Experience at Masi Agricola, a prestigious winery known for its high-quality Amarone wines. Here, visitors can indulge in a guided tasting of several Amarone vintages, paired with local cheeses and cured meats to enhance the flavor experience. Masi also provides insights into the philosophy and techniques behind their winemaking, giving you a deeper understanding of what makes Amarone so special. The Amarone tasting usually costs around $50 to $75 per person, depending on the selection of wines included.

For a more hands-on experience, consider joining a cooking class paired with a wine tasting at Fattoria Pasqua. This family-owned winery offers workshops that combine traditional Italian cooking with wine education. Participants can learn to prepare classic Veronese dishes, such as Risotto all'Amarone, while discovering the best wine pairings for each dish. This immersive experience typically costs about $80 to $120 per person, which includes the cooking class, meal, and wine pairings.

Many wineries also host seasonal events where visitors can taste new releases, participate in grape harvesting, or enjoy themed dinners that celebrate local cuisine. These events provide a unique opportunity to meet the winemakers, ask questions, and gain insights into their craft. Prices for these events can vary but typically range from $40 to $100 per person, depending on the inclusions.

To maximize your wine tasting experiences, it's advisable to make reservations in advance, especially during peak tourist seasons. Many wineries offer private tours and tastings for small groups, which can enhance the overall experience and allow for more personalized attention from the staff.

In conclusion, touring local vineyards in Valpolicella to taste the famous Amarone and Valpolicella wines is an enriching experience that immerses you in the region's rich viticulture history. Learning about the winemaking process and attending tastings and workshops deepens your appreciation for Italian wines and connects you to the traditions that have shaped this remarkable region. Whether you are a seasoned wine enthusiast or a curious beginner, Valpolicella's vineyards promise unforgettable experiences that will enhance your understanding of Italian wine culture. As you savor each sip, you'll carry home not just bottles of exceptional wine, but also a wealth of knowledge and memories from your journey through one of Italy's most celebrated wine regions.

CHAPTER 10:

GET ACTIVE WITH OUTDOOR ADVENTURES

Hike The Scenic Trails Around Verona, Perfect For Nature Lovers

Hiking around Verona offers a remarkable way to explore the stunning natural landscapes surrounding the city, where rolling hills, lush vineyards, and picturesque views abound. The region's varied terrain presents numerous trails that cater to different skill levels, allowing both novice and experienced hikers to immerse themselves in nature. One of the most popular hiking destinations near Verona is the Lessinia Natural Park, which features a network of trails winding through the mountainous terrain of the Lessinia plateau.

The park is renowned for its breathtaking views, unique geological formations, and rich biodiversity, making it a perfect escape for nature lovers. The Sentiero dei Contrabbandieri is a particularly picturesque trail, stretching approximately 12 kilometers and taking around 4 to 5 hours to complete. This trail offers stunning panoramas of the surrounding mountains and valleys, and you might even encounter wildlife such as deer and various bird species.

A convenient starting point for accessing the Lessinia Natural Park is the village of Malga San Giorgio, which can be reached by car from Verona in about 45 minutes. Here, you'll find parking facilities, and local guides are available to provide information about the best trails suited to your interests and abilities. Entrance to the park is free, but consider bringing a picnic to enjoy at one of the scenic viewpoints along the trail.

For those looking for a more challenging hike, the Monte Baldo area is highly recommended. Known as the "Garden of Italy," Monte Baldo boasts diverse flora and offers breathtaking views of Lake Garda and the surrounding landscape. The Sentiero della Foce trail, which starts from Bardolino, is a popular choice and can be completed in about 3 to 4 hours.

Many hikers also take advantage of the cable car from Malcesine to the summit of Monte Baldo, which provides stunning aerial views as you ascend. Once at the top, you can choose from a variety of trails, ranging from easy strolls to more challenging hikes. The cable car costs around $15 for a one-way ticket, and it's best to check the schedule in advance, especially during peak tourist seasons.

To ensure a safe and enjoyable hiking experience, it's wise to wear proper footwear and bring plenty of water and snacks. Additionally, consider downloading hiking apps or maps to help navigate the trails.

Enjoy Cycling Along The Adige River For A Unique Perspective Of The City

Cycling along the Adige River presents a fantastic opportunity to see Verona from a unique perspective while enjoying the fresh air and beautiful scenery. The Adige River, which flows through the heart of the city, is bordered by a well-maintained cycle path that stretches for several kilometers, making it accessible for cyclists of all skill levels.

One popular starting point for your cycling adventure is the Piazza Bra, where you can rent a bike from local shops such as Bici & Baci or Bike Rental Verona. Rentals typically cost around $15 to $25 per day, and you can choose from a range of bikes, including city bikes, mountain bikes, and even electric bicycles for an easier ride. Be sure to bring your identification and a credit card for the rental process.

As you pedal along the river, you'll encounter several key landmarks and attractions, including the historic Castelvecchio, the impressive Ponte Scaligero, and the beautiful Giardino Giusti. The cycle path is primarily flat, making it an enjoyable ride, and there are plenty of opportunities to stop and explore the riverside parks and cafes along the way.

A highlight of cycling along the Adige is reaching Parco della Rimembranza, a scenic park featuring well-maintained paths, lush gardens, and picturesque picnic spots. This area is perfect for a break, where you can relax and enjoy the beautiful views of the river and the surrounding hills.

For those interested in a guided experience, consider joining a cycling tour that focuses on Verona's history and culture. Companies like Verona Bike Tour offer guided rides that explore both the city's landmarks and the natural beauty along the river. These tours typically last around 2 to 3 hours and cost about $50, including bike rental and a knowledgeable guide.

As you cycle, take time to appreciate the serene environment and the vibrant city life along the riverbank. Keep your camera handy, as you'll want to capture the beautiful views of Verona's skyline reflected in the water.

Participate In Seasonal Activities Like Skiing In The Nearby Alps During Winter

While Verona is renowned for its historic architecture and beautiful landscapes, it also serves as an excellent base for seasonal activities such as skiing in the nearby Alps during the winter months. The Dolomites, a UNESCO World Heritage site, offer some of the most breathtaking skiing experiences in Italy, with world-class resorts just a couple of hours' drive from the city.

One of the most popular ski destinations is Madonna di Campiglio, located approximately 150 kilometers from Verona. This charming alpine resort features over 150 kilometers of slopes suitable for all skill levels, making it a perfect choice for both beginners and experienced skiers. The resort typically opens for skiing in early December and continues through late April, ensuring plenty of opportunities to enjoy the snow.

For those traveling without equipment, several rental shops in the area provide everything you need, from skis to snowboards and appropriate winter gear. Rental prices usually range from $30 to $50 per day, depending on the type of equipment you choose.

Madonna di Campiglio also offers a variety of other winter activities, such as snowshoeing, sledding, and ice skating. If you're seeking a more leisurely experience, consider taking a scenic walk through the snow-covered landscapes or enjoying a warm drink at one of the local mountain huts, where you can sample delicious strudel and hot chocolate.

Another fantastic option for skiing is Val di Fassa, which features a wide range of slopes and stunning views of the Dolomites. The resort is accessible via a 2-hour drive from Verona, making it convenient for a day trip or a weekend getaway.

To reach these ski resorts, consider renting a car for flexibility or booking a guided tour that includes transportation. Many tour companies in Verona offer packages that include transportation, lift tickets, and sometimes even ski lessons, making it easy for visitors to enjoy a full day on the slopes without the hassle of planning logistics.

As winter descends upon Verona, the allure of skiing in the nearby Alps becomes an attractive option for outdoor enthusiasts. The combination of beautiful scenery, thrilling activities, and the chance to experience Italy's stunning alpine culture adds a new dimension to your visit. Whether you're hitting the slopes or enjoying the après-ski atmosphere in the charming mountain villages, skiing near Verona is an experience you won't want to miss.

In conclusion, hiking the scenic trails around Verona, cycling along the Adige River, and participating in seasonal activities like skiing in the nearby Alps are all fantastic ways to explore the natural beauty and outdoor adventures that this vibrant region has to offer. Each experience provides a unique perspective of Verona and its surroundings, ensuring that visitors leave with lasting memories and a deeper appreciation for this enchanting part of Italy. Whether you're hiking through lush landscapes, cycling along a serene river, or skiing down powdery slopes, the opportunities for adventure and exploration in and around Verona are boundless.

CHAPTER 11:

LEARN THE SECRETS OF LOCAL CRAFTS

Visit Artisan Workshops To See Traditional Crafts Being Made By Hand

Exploring artisan workshops in Verona is a unique way to immerse yourself in the rich cultural heritage of the city. The tradition of craftsmanship is deeply rooted in Verona, where skilled artisans have been preserving their techniques for generations. As you wander through the cobblestone streets, you'll come across numerous workshops that showcase a variety of traditional crafts, from pottery to glassmaking and leatherwork.

One of the most renowned areas for artisan crafts is the Verona Artisan Quarter, located just a short walk from the city center. Here, you'll find workshops dedicated to pottery, woodworking, and textile arts. Laboratorio d'Arte, for instance, is a popular spot that specializes in handmade ceramics. Visitors are welcome to observe the artisans at work, molding clay and painting intricate designs. The workshop is open Monday to Saturday, from 10 AM to 6 PM, and you can take guided tours that provide insights into the history of the craft and the techniques used.

Another fascinating place to visit is the Vetreria Artistica, where you can witness the ancient art of glass blowing. This workshop offers demonstrations of the glassmaking process, showcasing how molten glass is transformed into beautiful works of art. The artisans here are incredibly passionate about their craft, and their expertise is evident in every piece they create. Demonstrations typically take place daily at 2 PM and 4 PM, and a small fee of around $5 is charged for admission. After the demonstration, don't forget to browse their shop for unique glass pieces that you can take home as a souvenir.

Additionally, don't miss the opportunity to visit workshops that focus on traditional leather goods. Bottega del Cuoio is one such workshop, where skilled artisans create high-quality leather handbags, wallets, and belts. Here, you can see the entire process, from selecting the finest leather to cutting and stitching the final product. The shop also offers guided tours and hands-on experiences, allowing visitors to try their hand at basic leatherworking techniques. Classes are available for groups and are typically priced around $60, providing a fantastic opportunity to learn from masters of the craft.

Visiting these artisan workshops not only enriches your understanding of Verona's cultural heritage but also supports local artisans who rely on their skills to sustain their livelihoods. By engaging with them, you become part of a narrative that spans centuries, connecting the past with the present.

Join Workshops To Try Your Hand At Pottery, Glass Blowing, Or Leatherworking

Joining hands-on workshops in Verona offers a fantastic opportunity to dive deeper into the traditional crafts that the city is known for. These experiences allow you to learn from skilled artisans and try your hand at various techniques, such as pottery, glass blowing, and leatherworking, all while creating your own unique keepsakes to take home.

If you're particularly interested in pottery, Corsi di Ceramica is a renowned pottery studio that offers classes for all skill levels. Located in the historic center of Verona, this workshop welcomes beginners and experienced artists alike. Classes are typically held on Saturdays from 10 AM to 1 PM and cost around $40, including all materials. You'll learn essential techniques like hand-building and wheel throwing, and you'll leave with a piece of pottery that you've crafted yourself, adding a personal touch to your collection.

For those captivated by the art of glass blowing, the Murano Glass School offers unique workshops that allow you to learn this age-old technique. Although traditionally associated with Venice, Murano glass craftsmanship has a significant presence in Verona as well. In these workshops, which typically last about 3 hours and cost around $100, you'll work alongside expert glassmakers to create your own glass art. Sessions are available several times a week, and you'll witness firsthand how raw materials are transformed into delicate pieces of art. The joy of shaping the glass while it's still hot and malleable is an unforgettable experience.

Leatherworking is another craft that you can explore through workshops at Artigianato del Cuoio, a workshop dedicated to leather goods. Here, you can participate in a half-day workshop where you'll learn the basics of leathercraft, including cutting, stitching, and finishing techniques. The cost for this immersive experience is around $80, and by the end of the session, you'll have created a custom leather piece to take home. These workshops often fill up quickly, so it's advisable to book in advance, especially during the tourist season.

These workshops provide not only a creative outlet but also a chance to connect with local artisans who are passionate about their crafts. You'll find that each workshop is infused with the rich cultural heritage of Verona, making it a meaningful experience that transcends typical tourist activities.

Discover The Importance Of These Crafts In Verona's Culture And Economy

The artisan crafts of Verona are more than just beautiful objects; they are a vital part of the city's cultural identity and economic landscape. The traditions of pottery, glass blowing, and leatherworking reflect the history of the region and contribute significantly to the local economy. As you explore these crafts, it's essential to understand their historical significance and the role they play in modern Verona.

Historically, artisans in Verona have been responsible for creating functional and decorative items that not only served daily needs but also expressed the artistic spirit of the region. The skills passed down through generations are a testament to the community's dedication to preserving its cultural heritage. For instance, the art of glass blowing, which has roots in ancient Rome, has evolved into a vibrant tradition that continues to thrive in Verona and its surroundings. The glass produced here is not only a local treasure but is also sought after worldwide, boosting the local economy through exports.

In recent years, there has been a renewed interest in supporting local artisans and promoting traditional crafts. The city has recognized the economic potential of artisan workshops and their ability to attract tourists looking for authentic experiences. This has led to initiatives aimed at promoting artisanal products, encouraging collaborations between artisans and local businesses, and hosting events like Verona Artisan Week, where local craftspeople can showcase their work. These events help raise awareness about the importance of handmade goods and the stories behind them, allowing visitors to appreciate the craftsmanship and effort that goes into each piece.

Moreover, the artisan crafts sector creates jobs and sustains the livelihoods of many families in Verona. Workshops not only employ artisans but also provide opportunities for apprenticeships, ensuring that traditional skills are passed on to the next generation. By participating in workshops and purchasing local crafts, visitors contribute directly to the local economy, helping to keep these traditions alive.

In summary, the artisan workshops in Verona offer more than just a glimpse into traditional crafts; they provide a deeper understanding of the city's cultural identity and economic landscape. By engaging with these artisans, joining workshops, and exploring the importance of these crafts, visitors can appreciate the rich history and vibrant community that define Verona. This connection to the past and present is what makes a visit to these workshops truly special, transforming a simple trip into a meaningful experience that celebrates the beauty of craftsmanship.

CHAPTER 12:

EXPERIENCE VERONA BY NIGHT

Explore The Vibrant Nightlife With Its Lively Bars, Pubs, And Clubs

Verona's nightlife offers an exciting blend of lively bars, charming pubs, and energetic clubs that cater to diverse tastes. As the sun sets, the city transforms, inviting both locals and visitors to experience its vibrant after-dark scene. Whether you're looking to sip on a cocktail at a trendy bar or dance the night away at a club, Verona has something for everyone.

The Piazza delle Erbe is a popular starting point for those looking to dive into the nightlife. Surrounded by stunning historic architecture, this lively square is filled with bustling bars and cafes. One must-visit spot is Cafè Al Teatro, a local favorite known for its exquisite cocktails and lively ambiance. Here, you can unwind with a drink while enjoying the view of the ancient market square. The bar is open until 1 AM, making it a perfect place to kick off your evening. Their signature cocktail, the Spritz, is a refreshing choice that embodies the essence of Italian aperitivo culture, priced at around $8.

For those who prefer a more relaxed atmosphere, Osteria Bar Al Pompiere offers a cozy vibe with an extensive wine list featuring local Valpolicella wines. This charming osteria is known for its welcoming atmosphere and delicious tapas, making it a perfect spot for a casual dinner before a night out. Open until midnight, the establishment serves dishes like Tagliere di Salumi for about $15, paired wonderfully with a glass of local wine.

As the night progresses, head to the vibrant Via Roma, where you'll find an array of clubs and dance venues. Alter Ego is one of the most popular nightclubs in Verona, renowned for its eclectic music selection and energetic dance floor. The club hosts a variety of themed nights, ensuring there's always something new to experience. Entry typically costs around $15, and drinks range from $8 to $12. With an open dance floor and frequent live DJ performances, this club is the perfect place to let loose and dance the night away.

If you're looking for something uniquely Veronese, check out Goccia. This stylish rooftop bar offers stunning views of the city skyline and is the perfect spot for a romantic night out. With a cocktail menu inspired by local ingredients, you can enjoy drinks like the Raspberry Prosecco Spritz while taking in the breathtaking scenery. Reservations are recommended, especially during peak season, and the bar is open until 2 AM.

Verona's nightlife truly comes alive after dark, providing an exciting array of venues to explore. From lively bars to energetic clubs, you can tailor your night out to suit your preferences, all while immersing yourself in the vibrant atmosphere that makes Verona a fantastic destination for nighttime fun.

Attend Outdoor Concerts Or Events That Showcase Local Talent

In addition to its lively nightlife scene, Verona is renowned for its outdoor concerts and cultural events that showcase local talent. The city has a rich artistic heritage, and throughout the year, various festivals and performances take place, celebrating music, theater, and dance. These events not only provide entertainment but also offer a glimpse into the creative spirit of Verona.

One of the highlights of Verona's cultural calendar is the Estate Teatrale Veronese, a summer festival that features a variety of performances, including concerts, theatrical productions, and dance shows. Held in iconic venues such as the Verona Arena, this festival attracts both local and international artists. The arena, a UNESCO World Heritage site, provides a stunning backdrop for performances, creating a magical atmosphere that enhances the experience. Tickets for concerts typically range from $20 to $100, depending on the artist and seating choice. It's advisable to book in advance, especially for popular performances, as they often sell out quickly.

For those looking to enjoy live music in a more intimate setting, Piazza dei Signori frequently hosts free outdoor concerts featuring local bands and musicians. These events create a lively atmosphere, and attendees can enjoy a diverse range of music styles, from traditional Italian folk to contemporary pop. Check the local events calendar for specific dates and times, as these concerts usually take place during the summer months and early fall.

Another fantastic event to experience is the Verona Jazz Festival, held annually in late spring. This festival celebrates jazz music with performances from talented local and international artists. Concerts take place in various picturesque locations throughout the city, including outdoor venues like Giardino Giusti and historical sites such as the Castelvecchio Museum. Admission prices vary, with some events being free and others requiring a ticket purchase, typically ranging from $10 to $30. This festival not only showcases incredible music but also fosters a sense of community as locals and visitors come together to enjoy the performances.

In addition to music events, Verona also hosts cultural fairs and food festivals that celebrate local cuisine and artisanal products. These events often feature live cooking demonstrations, tastings, and workshops led by local chefs and artisans. One such event is the Festa del Riso held in the spring, where visitors can sample a variety of rice dishes, including the famous Risotto all'Amarone, while enjoying live music and entertainment.

Attending outdoor concerts and events in Verona allows you to engage with the local community while experiencing the rich cultural heritage of the city. From the grandeur of the Verona Arena to the intimate charm of piazzas, these performances create lasting memories and foster a deeper appreciation for the artistic spirit of Verona.

Enjoy Romantic Evening Strolls Through The Illuminated Streets Of Verona

As night falls, Verona transforms into a magical setting, with its historic streets and landmarks illuminated, creating a romantic atmosphere that is perfect for evening strolls. Exploring the city at night allows you to appreciate its beauty from a different perspective, as the warm glow of street lamps and soft lights highlight the stunning architecture and vibrant ambiance.

Starting your evening walk at Piazza delle Erbe is a wonderful way to immerse yourself in the charm of Verona. This picturesque square is surrounded by historic buildings, and the market stalls, which are often still open in the evening, create a lively atmosphere. As you stroll through the piazza, take a moment to admire the beautiful frescoes on the surrounding buildings and the iconic Torre dei Lamberti, which stands tall at the corner of the square. Climbing to the top of the tower during the day offers breathtaking views of the city, but seeing it illuminated at night is equally enchanting.

From Piazza delle Erbe, you can make your way to the Piazza dei Signori, another stunning square that showcases Verona's historical significance. Here, you'll find the majestic Statua di Dante and the impressive Palazzo della Ragione. The square is often quieter in the evening, making it an ideal spot to pause and take in the serene surroundings. The buildings are beautifully lit, creating a romantic ambiance perfect for a couple's stroll.

As you continue your walk, head towards the Adige River. The riverside promenade is lined with trees and benches, offering a peaceful retreat from the bustling city. The view of the illuminated Ponte Pietra bridge, one of Verona's oldest bridges, is a must-see. Crossing the bridge gives you a fantastic view of the city reflecting on the water, providing a perfect backdrop for memorable photos. It's a great spot to sit and enjoy the sound of the flowing river while savoring a gelato from a nearby shop.

For those looking for a more intimate experience, consider a stroll up to Castel San Pietro, which provides stunning panoramic views of Verona, especially at sunset. The castle is open until 9 PM, giving you ample time to explore the grounds and soak in the beauty of the city as the lights begin to twinkle. The view from here is breathtaking, and it's a perfect spot to capture the essence of Verona as the day transitions into night.

Finally, end your romantic evening with a visit to one of the charming gelaterias or cafes scattered throughout the city. Enjoying a gelato while wandering the illuminated streets of Verona creates a magical end to your evening. Places like Gelateria Suso or Patisserie Azzini are local favorites, serving delightful treats that are perfect for a late-night snack.

Strolling through the illuminated streets of Verona is not just a walk; it's an experience that encapsulates the romance and charm of this beautiful city. The combination of stunning architecture, vibrant squares, and serene riverside views creates an enchanting atmosphere that lingers in your memory long after your visit.

CHAPTER 13:

YOUR ULTIMATE 6-DAY VERONA ITINERARY

Discover The Perfect Itinerary To Make The Most Of Your Time In Verona

As you embark on this exciting six-day journey through Verona, prepare to immerse yourself in the rich tapestry of history, culture, and stunning landscapes that this enchanting city has to offer. From the captivating sights of ancient Roman architecture to the delightful flavors of local cuisine, this itinerary is designed to ensure that you experience the very best of Verona. Each day is carefully curated to blend iconic landmarks with hidden gems, allowing you to soak in the atmosphere and get a true sense of the city. You will have the opportunity to stroll along picturesque streets, savor delicious dishes, and discover the warmth of Veronese hospitality. Pack your bags, put on your walking shoes, and get ready for an unforgettable adventure in one of Italy's most romantic cities.

Day 1: Arrival in Verona

Morning: Explore Piazza Bra and the Arena

Start your Verona adventure in Piazza Bra, the largest square in the city and a hub of activity. As you arrive, take a moment to admire the stunning architecture that surrounds you, including the impressive Verona Arena, a Roman amphitheater that dates back to 30 AD. Before heading inside, enjoy a leisurely breakfast at a nearby café, such as Caffè Al Teatro, where you can indulge in a traditional Italian pastry paired with a rich espresso.

After breakfast, head over to the Arena for a guided tour. The Verona Arena is one of the best-preserved Roman structures in the world, and exploring its vast interior is a must. Depending on the time of year, you may even get the chance to catch a rehearsal or performance. Spend about two hours soaking in the history and grandeur of this ancient monument.

Afternoon: Stroll Through the Historic Center

Next, take a leisurely stroll through Verona's charming historic center. Head towards Via Mazzini, a bustling shopping street lined with boutiques and cafes. This pedestrian-friendly avenue leads you to Piazza delle Erbe, the heart of Verona's market district. Here, you can browse local produce and handicrafts or simply enjoy a gelato while soaking in the lively atmosphere. Don't forget to snap a photo of the iconic Torre dei Lamberti, which you can climb for panoramic views of the city.

For lunch, stop at Osteria Al Duca, a quaint eatery known for its delicious pasta dishes. Try the Tortellini di Valeggio, a local specialty that is sure to please your palate.

Evening: Dinner and a Night Walk

As the sun begins to set, make your way to the Castelvecchio, a medieval fortress that houses an impressive collection of art. Explore the museum and walk along the scenic bridge, Ponte Scaligero, to catch a beautiful sunset view over the Adige River.

For dinner, dine at Ristorante Il Desco, where you can savor seasonal dishes inspired by traditional Veronese recipes. After dinner, take a romantic evening stroll along the riverbank. The soft glow of street lamps reflecting on the water creates a magical ambiance that is perfect for your first night in Verona.

Day 2: Discovering Verona's Art and Culture

Morning: Visit the Juliet's House and Museum

Begin your day with a visit to the famous Casa di Giulietta, or Juliet's House. Here, you can see the iconic balcony that inspired Shakespeare's tale of Romeo and Juliet. Take some time to explore the museum and learn about the legends surrounding this romantic story. Don't forget to leave a note on the wall, joining countless others in sharing your own love message.

Afterwards, grab a coffee at Caffè Romeo nearby and enjoy the lively atmosphere of this charming area. The café offers a range of delicious pastries and fresh coffee to kick-start your day.

Afternoon: Visit the Basilica of San Zeno

After your coffee, head to the Basilica of San Zeno, one of Verona's most important churches. The stunning Romanesque architecture and beautifully preserved artworks make this site a highlight of your trip. Spend some time admiring the intricate details of the altar and the stunning crucifix by Giovanni Bellini.

For lunch, stop at Trattoria Al Pompiere, which is famous for its local dishes. Try the Pastissada de Caval, a traditional horse meat stew that is a must-try in Verona.

Evening: Attend an Outdoor Performance

As evening approaches, prepare to experience Verona's vibrant cultural scene. Depending on the time of year, check the schedule for performances at the Verona Arena or other outdoor venues in the city.

Enjoy a live opera or concert, letting the enchanting music fill the air around you.

After the show, indulge in a late dinner at Ristorante 12 Apostoli, known for its creative twists on traditional Italian cuisine. Savor the local wine selection to complement your meal.

Day 3: Day Trip to Lake Garda

Morning: Travel to Lake Garda

On your third day, take a short trip to Lake Garda, just a short bus or train ride from Verona. The scenic views of the lake surrounded by mountains are truly breathtaking. Once you arrive in Sirmione, explore the charming town, known for its picturesque streets and beautiful shoreline.

Begin your day with a visit to the Scaliger Castle, a well-preserved medieval fortress that offers panoramic views of the lake. Spend about an hour wandering through its towers and enjoying the stunning scenery.

Afternoon: Relax by the Lake

For lunch, enjoy a meal at a lakeside restaurant like Ristorante Il Girasole, where you can savor fresh fish dishes and local wines while overlooking the water. After lunch, take some time to relax on the lakeshore or rent a boat to explore the lake at your own pace.

In the afternoon, don't miss the opportunity to visit the Grotte di Catullo, the ruins of a Roman villa situated on the peninsula of Sirmione. The views from this site are simply spectacular, and the surrounding gardens offer a lovely place to stroll.

Evening: Return to Verona

Head back to Verona in the late afternoon and refresh yourself at your hotel. For dinner, enjoy a cozy meal at Ristorante Osteria Rivel. Their rustic decor and traditional dishes create a warm and inviting atmosphere.

After dinner, take a stroll through the historic streets of Verona and enjoy the lively nightlife. Consider stopping by a wine bar like Enoteca Cangrande to sample local wines and engage with friendly locals.

Day 4: Wine Tasting in Valpolicella

Morning: Journey to Valpolicella

On day four, prepare to indulge in one of Italy's most renowned wine regions, Valpolicella. After breakfast, rent a car or join a guided tour to explore the vineyards and picturesque landscapes. Your first stop will be Villa della Torre, a beautiful villa that dates back to the 16th century. Take a guided tour of the estate and enjoy a wine tasting of their exquisite Amarone wines.

Afternoon: Lunch and Vineyard Tours

After your tasting, head to Trattoria Da Ruggero for a delicious lunch featuring local dishes paired with Valpolicella wines. The restaurant offers a cozy atmosphere and a menu that highlights the flavors of the region.

Following lunch, visit another vineyard, such as Corte Giara, known for its welcoming tours and tastings. Learn about the winemaking process and the region's rich viticulture history as you stroll through the vineyards and taste some of their best selections.

Evening: Dinner in Valpolicella

As the sun begins to set, enjoy a leisurely dinner at Ristorante Il Pigneto, known for its beautiful terrace overlooking the vineyards. Treat yourself to a traditional Veronese dish like Risotto all'Amarone, perfectly paired with a glass of local wine.

After dinner, return to Verona for a restful night at your hotel, reflecting on the wonderful experiences of the day.

Day 5: Nature and Relaxation

Morning: Hike in Lessinia Natural Park

On your fifth day, take a break from the city and immerse yourself in nature by visiting the Lessinia Natural Park. Located just a short drive from Verona, this park offers stunning landscapes, hiking trails, and the chance to see local wildlife. Pack a picnic lunch to enjoy amidst the beautiful surroundings.

Spend the morning hiking one of the many trails, such as the Monte Baldassarre trail, which offers breathtaking views of the surrounding valleys. This moderate hike takes about two to three hours, so be sure to wear comfortable shoes and bring plenty of water.

Afternoon: Explore the Park's Charm

After your hike, find a scenic spot to enjoy your picnic lunch while taking in the beauty of the park. Once you've recharged, explore the charming villages within the park, such as S. Anna d'Alfaedo, where you can visit local artisan shops and perhaps pick up some handmade souvenirs.

In the late afternoon, head back to Verona and take some time to relax at your hotel or enjoy a spa treatment at one of the local wellness centers.

Evening: Dinner in Verona

For dinner, indulge in a meal at Antica Bottega del Vino, a historic wine bar that offers a cozy atmosphere and an impressive selection of wines. Be sure to try their Baccalà Mantecato, a traditional dish made with salted cod, as you toast to a day filled with natural beauty.

After dinner, enjoy a leisurely evening walk through the streets of Verona. The soft glow of the city lights against the backdrop of historical landmarks makes for a romantic atmosphere, perfect for reflecting on your day.

Day 6: Departure and Last-Minute Discoveries

Morning: Visit the Giardino Giusti

On your final day in Verona, make sure to visit the Giardino Giusti, a beautiful Renaissance garden known for its stunning landscaping and impressive views of the city. Spend your morning wandering through the lush gardens, admiring the sculptures, fountains, and manicured hedges. This peaceful oasis offers a perfect backdrop for some final photos and moments of reflection.

Afternoon: Final Lunch in Verona

For your last meal in Verona, head to Ristorante La Finestra for a farewell lunch featuring local delicacies. Order a plate of Lasagna Veronese or Bigoli with Duck Sauce, paired with a glass of Valpolicella wine to savor the flavors of the region one last time.

Evening: Depart Verona

After lunch, take some time to do any last-minute shopping or sightseeing. Consider visiting the Arche Scaligere, the ornate tombs of the Scaliger family, or the Basilica di Santa Anastasia with its stunning frescoes.

As your time in Verona comes to an end, head back to your accommodation to collect your belongings. Reflect on the unforgettable experiences you've had over the past six days, from exploring ancient sites and indulging in local cuisine to savoring the beauty of the surrounding countryside. As you depart this enchanting city, carry with you the memories of Verona and the warmth of its culture, knowing you've experienced the very best that this remarkable destination has to offer. Whether you're planning to return or exploring new horizons, Verona will always hold a special place in your heart.

Made in the USA
Las Vegas, NV
06 February 2025